Word Bully

poems by

Clela Reed

Finishing Line Press
Georgetown, Kentucky

Word Bully

Copyright © 2018 by Clela Reed
ISBN 978-1-63534-579-7 First Edition
All rights reserved under International and Pan-American Copyright Conventions. No part of this book may be reproduced in any manner whatsoever without written permission from the publisher, except in the case of brief quotations embodied in critical articles and reviews.

ACKNOWLEDGMENTS

The author wishes to thank the editors of the following journals and presses where these poems first appeared: *Southern Poetry Review*—"Silent Letters," *Verse Virtual*—"Technicalities," *Valparaiso Poetry Review*—"Farrowing," Brick Road Poetry Press (*Dancing On the Rim*)—"Fallen Fruit," Pudding House Press (*Of Root and Sky*)—"Sea Snakes," "Time," "Definition," "Catalpa."

For generous insight and feedback on these poems, my sincere thanks to Rebecca Baggett, Sara Baker, Sarah Gordon, Emily Hipchen, Betty Littleton, Mary Anne O'Neal, Lee Ann Pingle, and Lisa Reeves, my poetry posse.

Thanks also to friends and family who have offered encouragement and support: Robert Ambrose, Gene Bianchi, Brenda Poss, Diane and Joe Riley, Shelly Corgel, William Dyess, Gregory Dixon, Linda Ames, and Barbara and John Schell.

For his excellent first readings, his fine suggestions, and for humoring my humor, loving thanks to my husband Lee.

Publisher: Leah Maines
Editor: Christen Kincaid
Cover Art: Lee Reed
Author Photo: Lee Reed
Cover Design: Elizabeth Maines McCleavy

Printed in the USA on acid-free paper.
Order online: www.finishinglinepress.com
also available on amazon.com

Author inquiries and mail orders:
Finishing Line Press
P. O. Box 1626
Georgetown, Kentucky 40324
U. S. A.

Table of Contents

Decision	1
On the Path	2
Farrowing	3
Sea Snakes	4
Letter Perfect	5
Lunar Effect	7
Metla	8
Morning Break	10
Garden Gossip	11
Word Bully	12
Fallen Fruit	13
Silk	14
Love Note	15
Time	16
Base Eight	17
Many Happy Returns	18
Silent Letters	19
Q	20
Digraphs	21
Plein Air Poets	22
However	24
Definition	25
Technicalities	26
Catalpa	27

Decision

Routine, that old, heavy stone,
holds me to the earth,
keeps me sensible and dull.
I'm tired of its weight in my arms.
I've decided to place it under the brittle leaves
of my old camellias who let the insects feed
and ignore the April frost that browns their buds,
settle it there where patient soil hums
with the monotonous wheel of seasons.

And then I'll turn away, light as a mote of dust
on shafts of light, iridescent, amorphous,
but clever enough to lecture dragonflies
and sing to the toads, to summon words
like playmates, invent a game for them,
arrange them, rearrange, wink,
grin the grin of fools,
and declare myself a poet.

On the Path

Acorns and shining berries
everywhere on the winding trail
through the darkened woods.
Crunching and mashing beneath each step,
strewn beyond each turn
like petals for a bride,
they took over my dream of—what?
I don't remember.

But they stay with me after waking,
to beg for meaning
        through their number,
        through the power of the vision.

Laughing, my writer's Muse,
absent too much lately,
whispers enlightenment,
but I can't quite catch her words,
which become the wind
in the highest leaves—quick
and gone.

I resort then to facts and association.
        Nuts as seeds
        and nourishment,
        pits within fruit,
        beginnings,
        stain from berries,
        tincture ... *ink*.
        Ahhh.

No wonder my Muse is amused.

Farrowing

I cupped my palm, squeezed tight
my fingers into a cone, and eased them
deep into the bulging hole.
My mother's voice coaxed me,
the one with the smallest hand.

Finding the piglet in the heaving sow
was harder than one might imagine,
what with the position, the stench,
the up-to-the-elbow awkwardness,
as I searched inside for a snout, a hoof,

something I could gently tug or turn
to solve the complication, a block
in the litter's flow, that ragged pace
of a dozen or more, slopped out,
scooped up, and placed gray and damp

like pedestrian words into lighted boxes.
But I always found them and was glad
to hear their piccolo squeals rising above
the sow's bass grunts as the piglets
warmed, grew pink with the effort of rooting

until the last arrived and suckling could begin.
It happened more than once,
farrowing troubles with a first delivery
or a breech or with tangled limbs
I'd need to turn and unravel.

And the struggle is still familiar—
the great sigh at the slick unlocking,
words spilling out at last in the rush of birth,
wet and new, warming up to life
and demanding to be heard.

Sea Snakes

Lines wait for me somewhere,
like those sea snakes in Fiji,
all the strong, fine lines
I'm sure to write someday.

Sleeping under gray skies at dawn,
slick and still as the shore rocks that
encircle them, precisely patterned
in the shallow water, they wait.

My camera flash springs
the inert coils into lines
of black and silver, pulsing,
then retreating with such shyness

that I'm amazed to later learn
of their potent venom,
more toxic than a rattler's,
but carried in docile fangs

to be used only when it matters,
effect being everything.

Letter Perfect

I want to give you a word,
your special one, all yours.

Choosing it will be my terrible task of love,
and I'll need several days, maybe a month,
to find this greatest gift, to sift through
the piles I pour all at once
onto the dining room table

where I'll search while the sun
makes its winter arc
low enough to send rays all day
through the southern windows
onto that tangle of serifed letters.

I'll drink oolong or orange-spice tea
and wear my old navy sweater
sprinkled with cat fur. I'll hum a few tunes
and at times smile, but I'll frown, too,
deep in lexiconcentration

as I consider and discard,
sort and assemble
stacks of syllabic clusters,
heaps of dictionary droplets,
trying to find your perfect word,

the one that fits precisely,
the one that you'll wear
on your honored being.
I can see it now,
that gift from me to you

pinned on like a boutonniere
or dangling from your pocket
on a chain
or—oh, yes, yes!

on your *lips*
as you repeat it again and again
smiling in between.

Lunar Effect
~ for Lana

When I was eleven the moon transformed.
No longer what the cow jumped over
or a Swiss cheese cartoon or a dusty
science fair model, it became personal,
for that's when I saw Disney's Annette

on our new Zenith television set,
lean from her window black-and-white,
and sing in sweetness flat as a lunar mare,
"Oh, Mr. Moon up above,
how will I know my love?"

My first child's child at eighteen months
discovered the bright ball or crescent,
and now points a tiny finger to the sky,
day or night, looking back as though to
claim our witness or ask that we fetch it.

"Moo, moo!" she learned to say at first,
eyes shining wide with wonder,
but after our son stressed the ending,
she now says, "Moo-nuh, Moo-nuh!"
a baby step from lyrical "Luna."

My imagination lifts off to orbit
her future, observe her moon's
incarnations, the spilling cycles and magic
of renewal, the lonely lamp, the pull
of tender tides, the fullness and the cusp.

Smart girl, she'll grasp the satellite
of cold mineral and science, but I hope
she'll hold the wonder, too, and
lean from her window one restless night
to sing her question to the moon.

Metla
> *~for Jimmy*

Once I visited a broom factory in Romania;
it was just as you'd imagine—
the cutting and sanding of sticks into handles,
the twine binding of straws.
But such pride! The owner and few workers
presented the brooms like bouquets,
watching our eyes for approval, honoring us
with little whisk favors to take home.
The humble tool of tidy shops and cottages
enjoyed an elevation in my eyes.

But not as much as today,
as my toddler grandson laser focuses
on brooms. Any brooms.
Kitchen brooms, industrial brooms,
hearth brooms, shop brooms—
all are here just for him, chubby arms out-stretched,
running diaper-bowlegged toward the prize.
"Metla, metla," he exclaims
in his mother's Macedonian. He squeals
at pictures of them in his favorite books,
searches for them in closets and garage,
drags them behind him, grips one
in each hand like a tiny skier,
and shoots them down the stairs
ahead of him with glee.

We scratch our heads and laugh.
What to make of such obsession?
I ignore jokes of profession and prefer
to think he's just learning like our earliest
kin that hands are meant to handle,
that wielding tools can shape our world,
and this swishing, sturdy, tall one

with nothing sharp nor rough,
but a means of pushing things about
seems a very good place to start.

Morning Break

My Should Bee is in the roses again,
lolling about on the big fragrant petals,
making a desultory pass
        at filling her leg baskets
though the field of wild flowers over the hill
and the patch of clover at roadside
offer more pollen.
        She's read the dances.

But how much lovelier here
on this pedestal atop a sturdy stem
unlike the wispy ones of poppies
and daisies that keep her bobbing
as she makes her worker rounds.
And the chance of being diced
in a mower or trampled by a bull
always threatens over there.
My Should Bee has reasons and prefers
at times to be a Could Bee or a May Bee.

My Should Bee knows
        the joy of *dis*orientation
as she sinks into the velvet,
replaces the buzz with a hum,
and imagines,
        for one full-blown moment
(dizzy with loyal drones)
that she is Queen.

Garden Gossip

Daisy rode and thyme wears on,
so thistle dew for now,
buttercup still overflows
when tulips meet to sip.
Lilac splendor on the chaise
since Flora's sweet tea rose
well before the white cows slip
and ladies' slippers yearn to skip.

Aster for the blue bell's ring
'fore Holly hocks the silver,
and forget-me-not at four o'clock
when cosmos turn with tea and talk
of nectar's theft and pollen's pilfer
and Queen Anne's lacey fling.

Word Bully

Words are my always-playmates
and I am the playground bully,
who prods, pokes, and bosses each phoneme,
letter-by-letter, into pouting submission.

At times I hand-join them with hyphens or send them
dashing—magic rope to guide them—to a promised
destination, only to find it wasn't there at olive!

When sufficiently cowed, words huddle together
(perhaps one should feel guilty) between parentheses
and make unnecessary comments under their breaths.
The ones who are superfluous (if the shoe fits,…)
are dismissed and they obviously know who they are,
for they've learned to drop a trail of crumbs
to find their way back.

When the mood strikes, I disimprove them
in puffy prefixes, attach shaggy suffixes to their rearments,
Crown Them with Capitals, or make them sit on hard,
black pavement just to show them off.
And if I'm *really* feeling testy,
I make them all stand leaning at an angle,
without touching one another
until recess is over.

Fallen Fruit: Variations on a Dream of Two Words

1. Fallen *Fruit*
always tastes better than that plucked from the limb—
all that warm, ripe flesh, of course, and peak-sweet juice
bleeding out the lusty past (petals embracing probing bee)
sealed within the flower's silent throat. And then the urgency
pricks. Before the wasp, worm, or clever deer arrives
to claim the easy prize; before wordless mouths
siphon up the tastes they cannot ¬name,
we'll gather the fruit at first light and hurry home.

2. *Fallen* Fruit
After Adam tasted the knowledgeable fruit,
after Persephone yielded to the pomegranate's seeds,
after Snow White bit into the poisoned apple,
what then? Oh, we know what happened to *them*,
but what about the fruit dropped, we can only assume,
with loathing? Did the tainted seeds swell within
the ignorant soil and sprout? then grow, blossom
to fruition in that juicy obscurity free of gods and demons?

3. *Fallen Fruit*
They're at it again, those two—pressing eye glands together,
sharing musk in their monogamous heat
—the Blue Duikers are kissing. So sweet.
Startled, they dash and careen
with all the grace of antelopean genes.
But here's the thing:
The very survival of the small ungulata
required evolution most strange,
for unlike other antelopes on the range,
these ruminates do not eat grass, and alas,
are much too small to reach fruit in trees, at all.
So they learned patience and stopped
looking up for their food,
feasting instead on fruit dropped,
full-ripened, unglued,
where it's easily found,
on reachable ground.

Silk

Say the word. Savor the sibilance
as the tongue approaches the teeth,
but withdraws coyly to the palate
to spool out the luxuriant fullness,
ending with the soft *kuh*.

Silk. Say it again and again,
and yards of shimmering fabric,
undulations of light,
rivers of color in shades of jewels
slip over your shoulders,
cling lightly to breasts
and skim the belly and hips,
to pool at your feet.

Silk. Say it again
and come to comprehend
the scandal, Plutarch dissuading
"the virtuous and prudent wife"
from wearing its near transparence,
the Senate's edicts
to prohibit such sensuality.

Say it quietly, *silk*.
Fabric of secrecy for centuries,
worn finally by Roman women
who dared to hide nothing.

Love Note

Take the "o",
sweet mouth
of mild surprise,
and crack it in two.
Balance the humps
atop the "v" next to it
and you have
a sloppy heart,
a comic valentine
to share
between the lanky "L"
of you
and the "e"
of me, with its one
good cyclopean eye
above
the happy grin.

Time

The "T" like
a sheltering tree,

> *(Every childhood has one—*
> *sentinel and friend*
> *with limbs like*
> *trusted arms.*
> *Mine had fragrant*
> *camphor berries*
> *and shiny leaves*
> *that flashed*
> *in sunlight*
> *all year long.*
> *And no matter*
> *where you found it,*
> *you made that tree*
> *your own.)*

the one that stood firm
all those years
as you struggled to learn
just who
the "i" and the "me"
who played beneath
would be.

Base Eight

That our fingers number ten
is what formed the base count then,
but had we sprouted eight;
four per hand would still operate
the tools and toys, would braid the hair,
crack the egg, slice the pear.
We really don't require all ten.

The thumb, of course, would surely win
most nondisposable, the old opposable
that made us all that we've become,
this handy, well-sucked plum
that gives us pinched precision,
that brings to fact a vision.

The pointer finger serves us well
as thumb's mate in show-and-tell
and fingers long enough for rings
and cupping close the fragile things,
strumming harps and banjo strings;
these workers we would miss,
but the pinky we could ditch.

We could do without that lazy fifth
extended at teacup, useless in lift.
Slender, unscarred, it stands at the side
a languorous princess, spoiled, untried.
Subtract those two then—
from the determining ten
and our base becomes eight!

Had that been our fate,
all would be subject to octification.
Octades of years and grim octimation,
Octinals in numbers and octigrams of gold,
and gold!—of Olympic greatness—
would only be given to those who showed
without compare their Perfect Eightness!

Many Happy Returns

Of all the letters on my keyboard,
only the R is wearing away.
Just half of it remains—
a P really, with loop lopped.
Should this be stopped?
And how did it happen?
Of course, all those robust words
like *ravishing, rushing*, and *rankle*
and the tender ones like *ripple* and *reticent*
I've probably used enough.
And how could I write poems
without *roots* and *ravens*?
How less tasty without *rhubarb*,
rum, and *remoulade*,
without the fragrance of *roses*
and *raspberries*,
the joy of *romp* and *ricochet*,
and the spunk of those
rascals and *rogues* who
pepper my verse?
Oh my! Just typing this poem
made it worse!
My ridiculous r-ification,
lines rife with r-ness.
Oh me! No wonder, no wond...
        Wait a minute, so what?
I know the key by touch
(left index visits it so much)
and will find it no harder to press
when it wears just a simple black dress.

Silent Letters

Aren't they tired of being silent?
Quaint guests (or captives) sitting there
like old maids at a wedding party,
prompting others' giggles when asked to dance,
don't they chafe at modern neglect,
those letters once shaped by ancient tongues
in hut and mead hall, their utterance
bellowed through whiskers and spit?

The cutting "k" of *know* and *knife,*
the guttural "gh" of *right* and *might,*
the final "e" of *fate, rite, mote,* and *brute,*
grace notes to the assaults of Saxon syllables.
So many, mute even when standing tall
like the "t" in *glisten, fasten* and *moisten.*
We've made them into ghosts—or glass.
We scarcely know they're there,
peering right through them to the
bustle of the street, the *thistle* in the garden.

Mourn for them, sounds once sung and said
by king and warrior, by bard and queen,
and ponder how we'd miss them
if they failed to take their place
at the noisy kitchen table
like shy kin or the very old, expected
to bow their heads for grace,
gnaw their biscuit, mind the crumbs.

Q

Oh, *Q. You*
must be the weakest sister
of the lot.
How can you not
want your own autonomy?
With *u* your constant escort,
you're quite the quivering quail.
Caught in your own quagmire
of quaint dependence, you
have too many questions,
too many qualms.
Quash your fears, girl! Quell your doubts!
Your quest is not quixotic!
Be the Queen!
the Qeen!

Digraphs

We've put them into counseling, the H brothers,
for they can't seem to help it,
glomming onto certain others
as they do, making sounds from the hell pit
of phonetic functioning—all wind and spit.
The p, the s, the t, the w—there's no resisting
embracing these letters in linguistic trysting.

What must they think—the Slavs and Latinos—
when teaching their deti and bambinos?
For such sounds in their language have separate letters.
And what about the Chinese and Congolese?
Can their complex letters allow for these?

Relics of an earlier age, the brothers are driven to engage
in such buddy bonding that we've tried to ignore them,
but maybe it's time to implore them
to stand on their own, bring in some marks diacritical
and make their digraphable laughable.

Plein Air Poets

In that coastal town atop celadon cliffs,
plein air poets arrive early, find the spot
that calls them beside the curving walk,
beneath the palms, above the aqua swirls
fringed in white. They stand their easels,
prop large Strathmore pads of paper,
and arrange markers or pens along the tray.
They stare out to sea; sometimes
they close their eyes and breathe deeply.
Some effect the fluorescent hum of industry.

Then they begin their plein air poems,
sketching in the first stanza quickly.
Passersby will often stop, linger
at a reverent distance to observe
the phenomenal skill, emit tiny sighs
like orgasmic hamsters at perfect line breaks,
specific details, the brilliant stroke of vivid verb.
They may even applaud a wise deletion,
or cluck their tongues at verse gone too free.

At times the plein air poet wishes conversation.
"These lines are just too muddy," he might say
as though to himself, shaking his head dramatically.
"Oh, not at all," says the paused jogger or
walker-of-dogs, "You paint a subtle abstraction."
The plein air poet frowns in thought, stares out to sea.

Once, it's told, a well-heeled stroller with fulsome
ego sauntered past several poets of an afternoon
before stopping suddenly at a plein air post
and declaring the poet a "discovery," a *mystic* whose work
must be brought to the masses. But this is only
a plein-air-poetry legend and likely never happened.

Finally, as the sun eases its cadmium orange body
into the bath of cerulean blue, the plein air poets

stare out to sea, pack up their crumpled sheets,
their sheaves of scribbled lyrics, their sonnets
and their odes, their yet-dripping confessionals,
and leave the park, certain they achieved something
worthy that day in the light that will never be repeated,
under skies as unique as they.

However

Welcomed in gutters, in bill baskets,
in roadway freedom at four a.m.
and long stretches of vacant beach
of any country in any season at dusk,
in medicine spoons and egg shells, it grins.

>*Empty* wants not,
>and sinks into an easy chair
>to savor satisfaction.

But it cries misery in the stomach,
the promise, the lagging bank account,
the gas tank, and sometimes the nest.
It bemoans the barren womb,
the blank page, the lead-gray sky.

>*Empty* stands tiptoed
>on meager feet to nose-press
>panes of plenty.

With yin-yang reasoning, then, even
a heart half empty has chance to thrive,
given hope's funnel
and love's full-moon tide.

Definition

Who wouldn't choke on the dust of denotation?
As though the heart were only a pump,
the moon a satellitic chunk.
How juicy raw sensation (fleshmind, mindflesh);
how true electric glue in folds of gray!

A sliver of light could encompass all hope,
and lust could arrive on the scent of an orange,
despair on the taste of the wind.
Inscrutable yet absolute, joy might be
spelled in wood smoke or goose down
or in warm mud-ooze between toes.

Ah, to dance in mists of nuance,
to paint with hinting shades until
the bleeding layers blend into design
and finally drench the thirsty vellum
that memory will frame.

And that painting becomes the meaning,
and that meaning becomes the life,
defined in strokes iconoclastic
by the floating petal, the pool of blood,
the gypsy's eye.

Technicalities

Because I cannot talk
to those who've left,
ears once primed to listen,
I talk instead to the world at large—

to cynical cities, wide-eyed towns,
to unknown selves
across the drifting plates
that bear the listening hills
and open steppes,
the woods alert to the charge of air
that shimmers leaves to attention.

Wireless warbler, I cyber sing and text.
I learn to tweet and blog.
I submit. I send.
I'm World's new Friend

as I e-chat clicking comments to the skies,
the stratosphere, beyond.
Who knows how far these signals go?
Sometimes I sense impossible replies,
messages I can never open
except in desperate dreams.
And even then the words
are enigmatic and the date
is never clear.

Catalpa

I asked him to write the word,
not just draw the leaf,
but the tattoo artist
at Pain and Wonder said he couldn't;
the letters were too small for him
though others were known for such skill.
I'll wait. Someday I'll have inscribed
along the curve of the leaf
I wear on my back
this word I love—its shape
a pleasing scape of lines and space,
closed in tight and opened wide,
two trunks above, a root below,
a crescent moon to the west.

And—even more, its *sound*.
Easy utterance, the "ca," which
even birds with no lips can say,
baby babble, soft from the back
of the mouth, my old familiar C
combines with ah, and then the "tal"
like the letter T and tree trunks
and telephone poles,
all tall and able, one signal of faith,
one pointer to the sky,
a stone to sit upon between,
followed, of course, by the gentle "pa,"
puff of breath, lips required,
affection with a tap root,
sometimes naming father and
especially fine for my own,
who worked among the trees,
a gentleman by nature.
For him I'll wear the leaf
in shape of a heart
just behind *my* heart
where words,

even one so pleasing,
are, after all, not needed.

Clela Reed left teaching in 2003 to write fiction, but kept returning to her old love, poetry. She lives and writes with her husband and too many deer in her woodland home near Athens, Georgia. She is the author of five collections of poetry: Books: *Dancing on the Rim* (Brick Road Poetry Press, 2009), *The Hero of the Revolution Serves Us Tea* (Negative Capability Press, 2014), based on her service in the Peace Corps in 2010-2011, and *Or Current Resident* (Kelsay Books, forthcoming 2018). Chapbooks: *Bloodline* (Evening Street Press, 2009) and *Of Root and Sky* (Pudding House Publications, 2010). She has had poems published in *The Cortland Review, The Southern Poetry Review, The Atlanta Review, Valparaiso Review, The Literati Review, storySouth Journal, Clapboard House Literary Journal,* and others. She has taught many workshops and has given readings or participated in them in several states and in St. Petersburg, Russia, and Oradea, Romania. During her Peace Corps service, she wrote weekly in a blog, www.clelainromania.blogspot.com.

www.ingramcontent.com/pod-product-compliance
Lightning Source LLC
LaVergne TN
LVHW041518070426
835507LV00012B/1663